TWICKENHAM, TEDDINGTON & HAMPTON

A SECOND SELECTION

MIKE CHERRY, KEN HOWE & JOHN SHEAF

SUTTON PUBLISHING LIMITED

Sutton Publishing Limited
Phoenix Mill · Thrupp · Stroud
Gloucestershire · GL5 2BU

First published 1998

Copyright © Mike Cherry, Ken Howe
and John Sheaf, 1998

Photograph page 1: St Alban's Church,
c. 1910.

British Library Cataloguing in Publication Data
A catalogue record for this book is available from the
British Library.

ISBN 0-7509-1695-8

Typeset in 10/12 Perpetua.
Typesetting and origination by
Sutton Publishing Limited.
Printed in Great Britain by
Ebenezer Baylis, Worcester.

ABOUT THE AUTHORS

Mike Cherry, Ken Howe and John Sheaf are very good friends who live in Twickenham, Teddington and Hampton respectively. they are all prominent members of the Borough of Twickenham Local History Society and participate fully in all its activities. They are authors, individually or jointly, of a number of books on local history including *Hampton and Teddington Past, Teddington Past and Present* and *Hampton in the 1890s – Through the Eyes of Captain Christie of Beveree*, pamphlets, papers and articles and give talks on various aspects of the area described in this book.

In addition, they are all founder members of the West London Postcard Club and have large collections of old photographs and postcards of their areas. They have collected this material for more than a decade and have selected some of the very best items to illustrate this book. Many of these pictures are rare, some unique, and nearly all have never been published in book form before.

The authors are also members of their local societies and amenity groups, and all take a great interest in the locality, its history and development, and in the preservation of the best of the past. They are particularly keen to broaden people's interest in the community and history of the area covered in the book and hope that it will encourage a greater awareness in, and knowledge of, the locality.

Readers who share some of all of the interests mentioned are encouraged to join the Borough of Twickenham Local History Society (which covers the Hamptons, Teddington and Whitton as well as Twickenham). The annual subscription is £6.00 and should be sent to the Membership Secretary, 86 Cole Park Road, Twickenham TW1 1JA.

CONTENTS

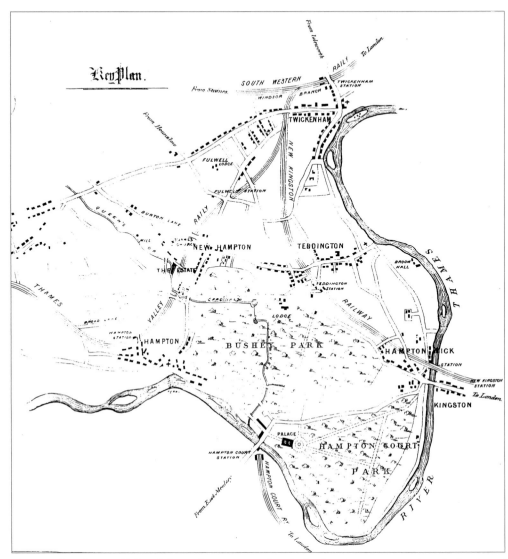

This map dates from *c.* 1868 and shows the area covered in the book as it was at approximately the time of the earliest photographs published here. Readers will be only too aware of the enormous development that has taken place since.

INTRODUCTION

We are very pleased to say that our first book in this series, published in November 1996, was well received, and as a result of this, we have been asked to prepare this second volume. Still covering the geographical area of the old Borough of Twickenham that was formed in 1937, we are pleased to present a further selection of pictures, mainly from the late Victorian and Edwardian eras. We have also tried to incorporate some later pictures, although ironically these are harder to find than their Edwardian counterparts. This is due in particular to the great postcard collecting habit that existed at the beginning of this century, which has meant that the contents of many Edwardian collections have survived.

Following the first volume, many people contacted us to agree or disagree with what we had said, to add more information to whatever was stated or to related matters, or simply to say that they had enjoyed the book. We found this both greatly enjoyable and rewarding and we would once again welcome any feedback, which should be sent c/o 75 Radnor Road, Twickenham, Middlesex TW1 4NB.

We hope that you will enjoy reading the book as much as we did preparing it.

Mike Cherry
Ken Howe
John Sheaf
November 1998

ACKNOWLEDGEMENTS

Once again we have received much help and support from our friends and colleagues, and in particular we would like to thank Vic Rosewarne for the captions on the Whitton pictures and some of the Twickenham shots. As usual Chris Turfitt and Jane Baxter of the Local Studies section of Twickenham Library provided help over and above the call of duty. The Greater London Borough of Richmond provided several of the Twickenham pictures. Roy Beale provided the photograph of his father's shop in Teddington. Victor Warden gave a photograph of Trafalgar School; Mrs Walby (née Helena Heavens) kindly loaned two Hampton pictures; Betty Barton, Gwen Tough, Avril Lansdell, Tony Cannings, Michael Beaney, Colin Pain, Robert Crewdson and the Teddington Society all supplied other much needed pictures. Arthur Fay filled in many blank areas from his Teddington collection. Peter Broadley gave his advice on Hampton Wick, and Tony Cannings and John Cook both expertly copied some of the pictures for us. Dick Cashmore offered his advice in several areas and the late Alan Urwin was a general inspiration for the project. Lastly Sharman Sheaf once again faced up to the daunting task of transcribing her husband's scrawl into the Hampton captions.

CHAPTER ONE

CENTRAL & NORTH TWICKENHAM

Russell's Corner, c. 1920s. William Russell had established a cycle shop on the corner of Church Street and Church Lane in about 1924. The location had been known as Mesley's Corner because it was home to a boot shop run by Maria Mesley from the 1870s to 1917. The Mesley family included a number of shoemakers in Twickenham. William Russell also owned the adjacent property in Church Lane (see overleaf). The corner area of Church Street was cleared in 1962 and now forms the Church Square development.

The junction of Church Street and Church Lane in 1962, on the day before demolition. Russell's Corner is on the right and the wall of St Mary's churchyard is to the left. The central timber-framed building was the Two Sawyers public house, in continuous use as licensed premises from at least 1737 until 1918. William Russell took over the building in about 1924 to accommodate his cycle and motor engineering business.

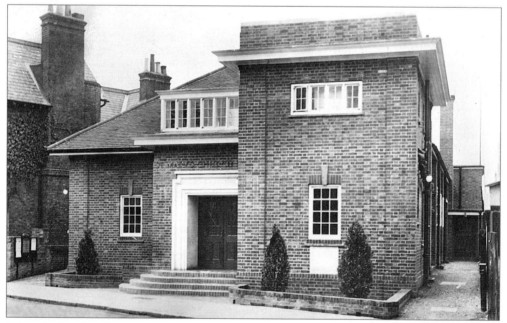

St Mary's Church Hall, Church Street. This hall was opened in 1933, on the site of an old scout hut, and marked the 600th anniversary of the first vicar of Twickenham. The hall was demolished to allow for the Civic Centre development which opened in 1990 and a new, and considerably more comfortable, hall replaces it. The old hall, however, had a small part to play in Twickenham's musical history as it was the venue in 1964 for the first performance by the band '1984', which was formed by Brian May who went on to become a member of the rock group 'Queen'.

St Mary's Church viewed from Church Alley, 1906. The early eighteenth-century houses to the left have survived threats of redevelopment in the 1950s and the area retains some of the character of this heart of the original village.

An interior view of St Mary's Church. This picture would have been taken no later than 1901 when the organ was moved from the position shown in the north gallery, to the south.

St Mary's Church and the Embankment, 1913. To the left is the Barmy Arms public house, then the Queen's Head. The Mission Room, partly obscured by the tree in the centre, was built in 1870 and now forms the Mary Wallace Theatre. The horse and cart behind the tree are from John Perring, the furnisher's, who had shop premises in the London Road.

The Embankment, 1932. The island ferry, the only means of access to Eel Pie Island until Snapper's Bridge was built in 1957, is in the foreground. To the left is the boathouse, previously Shore's, which Hammerton's had taken over in 1926.

Twickenham Boys' and Girls' Regatta, 1911. The boys are standing on the edge of a barge leaning on the greasy pole. The prize for the boy who could succeed in walking the length of the pole was the carcass suspended on the left. The houses in the left background were at the foot of Water Lane: they were damaged by bombing in the Second World War and subsequently demolished.

The Island Hotel, Eel Pie Island, *c*. early 1900s. The hotel looked out to the Ham bank of the Thames and reached the height of its popularity in the early years of this century.

The Island Hotel, *c*. early 1900s. This view from the Ham bank shows the dance hall which had been added to the hotel in 1898.

A view across King Street and down Church Street showing the decorations for Charter Day, 22 September 1926, when Twickenham became a municipal borough. The banner to the left on what is now Barclays Bank reads in full 'Success to our Borough'. The Charter Mayor was Dr John Rudd Leeson who lived at Clifden House (see page 42).

King Street, c. 1940s. The wide and, to the modern eye, traffic-free high street was created by road widening in 1927.

York Street, *c.* 1925. Moss Bros shop is on the left; Deayton's Stores, of which there were other branches in Twickenham and Teddington, are on the corner of York Street and Garfield Road.

Gernat's milliner's shop in 1908 with shop staff posing in the doorway. Street directories record an 'M. Gernat' milliner's shop at 62 York Street in the late 1920s and early 1930s but the precise location of the shop in 1908 remains uncertain.

Tomlin's Alley, 1936. Although the alley itself still exists, running from King Street alongside Woolworths to Holly Road, all the buildings in this picture have since gone. To the right is the Horse and Groom public house, which occupied part of Woolworths' site, and up to about 1890 the passage was known as Horse and Groom Alley. At that date there were a number of small houses on each side of the alley, one occupied by Richard Hammerton, a local waterman, together with his wife, four sons and three daughters.

The post office, London Road, c. 1908. It was opened in July 1908. To the extreme left is Perring's furnishings shop.

London Road, early 1900s. The Black Dog public house (currently the Hobgoblin) is behind the tram; Holly Road runs to the right behind Thomas's butcher's shop (with the canopy) with the Duke of York public house on the far side.

Fortescue House, London Road, early 1900s. Amyand Park Road (now Arragon Road) is to the right. Note the postman with his bicycle on the right.

The Railway Tavern, London Road, *c.* 1916. The pub was renamed the Cabbage Patch in the early 1960s after the name 'Billy Williams' cabbage patch', which had been given to the rugby ground in its early days. Brandon's was the local brewery supplying many of Twickenham's public houses, and was based just over the railway (Cole's) bridge where the postal sorting office now stands.

Twickenham railway station, 1924, from the railway bridge. Note the milk churns on the right-hand platform.

Twickenham station , early 1900s, from the junction of Station Yard and Queen's Road. The Albany Hotel is just out of the picture on the left behind the row of trees, of which now only one stump remains.

Construction of a replacement bridge in London Road over the railway, March 1965. The new bridge is on the extreme left. In the centre is the original Rugby Tavern in Railway Approach, which was demolished as part of the redevelopment.

The River Crane from Cole's Bridge, London Road, 1908, looking east. To the left are various buildings of Brandon's Brewery, now the sorting office. The brewery had been leased to Brandon's in 1892, having been in the Cole family since at least 1635 when Moses Glover's map shows 'Mr Thomas Coole, Brewer' on the site. To the right are the grounds of Heatham House.

Heathfield North, c. early 1900s. The area of Marsh Farm, on which Heathfields North and South and other roads were gradually developed, was prone to flooding from the River Crane. The precise date of this photograph is not known but there were floods in the area in 1892/3, 1895, 1903/4, 1914, 1916 and 1920.

Brook House, London Road, 1909. Thought to have been built in the early 1600s, the house had been much altered over the years, including the removal of one whole storey in 1829. Used at various times as a private school, the house was saved in 1953, along with neighbouring Neville House, from demolition, to make way for a new primary school. Brook House survived until the early 1960s when it was replaced by flats which retain the name.

The Cottage, London Road, 1910. Sited almost opposite the junction with Cole Road, The Cottage was, at the date of this picture, the home of Henry Lloyd who owned a chemist's shop at 1, Old Palace Terrace, Richmond Green. The house was demolished in 1939 to make way for a drill hall.

The Rugby Ground, 1963. Although a relatively recent photograph, the contrast of the modest scale of the spectator stands with today's stadium is striking.

The Twickenham Nightingale Home, 1907. Sited in Strafford Road, the home 'for the reception of paying patients and supply of hospital trained nurses' was under the supervision of Misses Uglow and Emmitt and at the date of this photograph had recently moved from 20 London Road to the Red House, 12 Strafford Road, later relocating to a house opposite.

Van Toll, Mayer & Co., Richmond Road, *c.* 1907. Johannes Van Toll was a Dutchman who came to England in the mid-1890s and in 1900 founded the Thames Valley Motor Co. Ltd and produced the 'New Orleans' car. Based on the Belgian 'Vivinus', the car was built at the Orleans Works, originally on the corner of Chapel and Orleans Roads and later at Sherland Road. The premises in Richmond Road have remained in use as a garage to the present day.

York House from the River Thames. This picture dates from before 1911 when the last private owner of York House, Sir Ratan Tata, had the stone bridge constructed joining the riverside gardens, laid out by the Duc d'Orléans in the 1890s, to the grounds of the house. The balustraded wall was part of the Duc's improvements.

Queen's College, c. 1906. Although identified on the photograph as in Amyand Park Road, records fail to show the precise location. However, up to about this date there was a Queen's College at nos 9–13 Queen's Road in Twickenham.

Sion Road on 8 May 1945 with flags flying to celebrate VE Day. The junction with Ferry Road is just past the building in the centre, then Weston's General Stores. An advertisement for 'Gold Flake' can be made out just below the window.

Twickenham ferry, *c.* 1905, from the Ham bank. Mount Lebanon, to the right, was built in the 1790s, its name deriving from the cedars in the grounds.

CHAPTER TWO

EAST TWICKENHAM &
MARBLE HILL

Orleans House, c. 1860s. This very early photograph from the Ham bank shows the main section of the house, built in 1710, and the low-lying riverside meadow. The Orléans connection dates from 1815 when Louis Philippe, Duc d'Orléans, was forced to leave France and retired to Twickenham where he had previously lived in exile at nearby Highshot House in Crown Road, from 1800 to 1807.

In contrast to the previous picture of Orleans House in its Victorian prime, this view of the north (Richmond Road) side dates from 1926 when demolition was under way to allow for gravel extraction, leaving only the Octagon, adjoining offices and the stables.

Marble Hill House, c. 1911. As befits a public park, there is a sign in the ground floor window advertising tea and coffee. The bowler-hatted gardener adds a touch of class to the park.

Sheep grazing in Marble Hill Park, *c.* 1907. In the background are buildings in what is now the Beaufort Mews development. The sheep represent a long tradition of livestock on the estate; the original owner, the Countess of Suffolk, had a farm and kitchen garden in the grounds, and prints from the nineteenth century show sheep and cattle grazing in the park.

Orleans Road, *c.* 1920s, looking towards the Richmond Road. Behind the figures to the right is the Phoenix Inn, which at this date had been converted to a private house.

The Phoenix Inn, Orleans Road, early 1900s. The first reference to the Phoenix Inn was in 1859, although a Phoenix Brewery is mentioned in 1851 in Chapel Row (the former name of Orleans Road), and it may date from the 1830s. Licensing records contain no reference after 1914, so it seems that the building became a private house during the First World War.

The Warren, early 1900s. The riverside walk between Orleans Road and Richmond Bridge, now known as Marble Hill footpath, took its earlier name of The Warren from the nearby site of a rabbit warren in the seventeenth century (and possibly earlier) in the estate later known as Cambridge Park. Rabbits were prized for their meat and fur and were farmed in enclosed mounds in the Twickenham area from the mid-thirteenth century, not long after their introduction to England.

Interior of the Church of St Margaret of Scotland, St Margaret's Road. It opened in 1938 and, although a temporary structure, was to last until 1969 when the present church was built.

Richmond Road, c. 1918. This view shows Crown Parade at the junction with Crown Road. On the left is James Maunders, confectioner's, and next door the shops of James Lawrence and Mrs K. Lawrence, furniture and wardrobe dealers respectively.

The bridge joining Beauchamp Road and Cole Park Road, late 1920s. This photograph was taken from the footbridge over the railway which joins Beauchamp Road (out of view on the other side of the railway to the left) and Cole Park Road (out of view to the right). The bed and banks of the River Crane are being concreted. In the distance are the buildings of Brandon's Brewery. The bridge was demolished in 1930.

William T. Twinn's stationer's and newsagent's shop, 12 Crown Road, 1926. The *Sunday Graphic*'s offer of '£5 a week for life free' is a pointed reminder of inflation over the last seventy years.

CHAPTER THREE

STRAWBERRY HILL

An aerial view of Strawberry Hill House and grounds, c. 1930s. Horace Walpole's original eighteenth-century Gothic house is towards the right of the picture with Lady Frances Waldegrave's nineteenth-century extension in the centre. The house became a teacher training college in 1927 and the college buildings form the left-hand half of the development.

Girls playing cricket in the grounds of St Catherine's Convent High School, *c.* 1932. The school occupied Pope's Villa from 1919 until 1996 when St James's School took over the riverside site.

The dining hall of St Catherine's School, *c.* 1920s.

Interior of Pope's Grotto, *c.* 1920s: this view of one of the chambers of the grotto has not changed since that time. The statue is thought to be of the Virgin Mary and is not part of Alexander Pope's original decoration. The bare walls of the grotto chamber were originally heavily decorated with glass, shells, ores and other unusual materials.

Cross Deep looking south towards Pope's Villa, *c.* 1909. To the left foreground are the gate piers of Cross Deep, surmounted by pineapple finials with a glass-roofed path to the house. The next building, fronting the road, is Riversdale, built in the late 1770s by George Shirley and known as 'Spite Hall' because it was thought to have been positioned deliberately to block the view from Crossdeep Lodge, which stood on the other side of the road. The tower of Pope's Villa can be seen in the distance.

Pope's Grove, *c*. 1920s. Apart from the absence of any traffic the view has changed little.

Pope's Avenue, *c*. 1923. Looking to the north, this photograph was taken before the flats, Wellesley Court, were built on ground behind the trees on the right.

Radnor House and gardens, early 1900s. To the right is Cross Deep Hall which, like Radnor House, was destroyed in the Second World War. The channel that effectively made the grounds of Radnor Gardens into an island runs behind the group of children.

The War Memorial, Radnor Gardens, early 1920s. The memorial was unveiled on 2 November 1921 and this picture was clearly taken shortly after an Armistice Day ceremony. The building to the right of the memorial is the ornamental boathouse in the grounds of Cross Deep Hall.

Poulett Lodge from the river, early 1900s. One of a sequence of substantial eighteenth-century riverside houses which lined Cross Deep, Poulett Lodge ended its days as the Newborough Club in the late 1920s (a subsequent venture to launch it as the Monte Carlo Sports Club failing) before demolition for the development of Thames Eyot.

Walpole Lodge, Waldegrave Road, 1914. This picture is typical of the postcard views of private houses taken by local photographers, in this case a photographer from Bedford Studios of 72 Waldegrave Road. Walpole Lodge stood between Southfield Gardens and Strawberry Hill Road.

Thurnby, at the junction of Wellesley Road and Spencer Road, early 1900s. One of several large Victorian houses in Wellesley Road, Thurnby, like Milton House and Wentworth House, is now remembered only in the name of the flats which have replaced it.

Strawberry Hill Road, 1924. The road was developed in the 1880s when much of the area was being sold for house building, following the death of Lady Frances Waldegrave in 1879, as part of the Waldegrave Park estate. The parked vehicle is from the Imperial Laundry in Kew Foot Road, Richmond.

Twickenham High School and School of Music, c. 1912, front view. The High School stood in the Hampton Road on the site where the present Archdeacon Cambridge's School was opened in 1968. One of the boarders in the 1920s was Dirk Bogarde, whose unsatisfactory school report led to his being moved to the stricter St Catherine's Convent School in Pope's Villa.

Archdeacon Cambridge's School, c. 1918. The school had been built in 1842 in Vicarage Road, adjacent to Holy Trinity Church which had been consecrated the previous year. The buildings were in continuous use until 1968 when the new infant and junior schools were opened in the Hampton Road. This photograph was taken from Pope's Avenue.

CHAPTER FOUR

WEST TWICKENHAM

The junction of Cross Deep (to the left) and King Street, with Heath Road, c.1870. Mann's Coach Builders occupy the ground floor of the centre building which replaced a much earlier house named The Grove, home of Francis Poulton, a lawyer who died in 1642; his memorial is in St Mary's Church. The building in the photograph was replaced by the Luxor cinema in 1929, renamed the Odeon in 1944, which closed in 1981. Only a section of the terrace on the extreme right still remains.

Havelock House, Heath Road, *c.* 1934. Probably dating from the eighteenth century, Havelock House had eight bedrooms, stabling, and gardens which ran alongside the passageway from Heath Road to Radnor Road. The profile of the roof line of Havelock House can still be made out today on the flank wall of Luxor Mansions. The photograph was probably taken just prior to demolition.

Savile House, Heath Road, *c.* 1904. Named after the widow of Sir George Savile, a late eighteenth-century resident, Savile House is best known as the home in the 1720s and 30s of Lady Mary Wortley Montagu, one-time close friend and later enemy of Alexander Pope who lived nearby in his Villa in Cross Deep. At about the time of this photograph there was a proposal to use the house as a Conservative and Unionist Club. Demolished in 1909, Saville (*sic*) Road marks the approximate site.

F. Witt's bakery, Heath Road, *c.* 1908. The Witt family traded as bakers on the north side of Heath Road from 1905 to 1919 when the business was taken over by Lawrence Jenkins.

Twickenham County School for Girls, Clifden Road, 1920s. The school opened in 1909 and became the Adult Education Centre in the early 1980s. A new wing was added in 1936 to the extreme left of the school in this picture.

Dr John Rudd Leeson, family and staff in the grounds of Clifden House, 1904. Dr Leeson, seen here standing by the garden bench, was a prominent Twickenham resident and local politician who was Charter Mayor in 1926 when Twickenham changed status from an Urban District Council to a Borough Council. Clifden House was built in 1886 and stood on the corner of Heath Road (to the left of this picture) and Clifden Road, the newly built houses of which can be seen on the right. The house was demolished in 1974; a magnolia tree from the front garden remains in front of the offices which were built on the site.

Twickenham Green, c. 1924. This view looks across the green to the Staines Road side, with people enjoying a warm spring day with the horse chestnut trees in blossom.

Holy Trinity Church, Twickenham Green, *c.* 1905. To the right of the church, in Vicarage Road, is Archdeacon Cambridge's School.

Celebrating Empire Day on Twickenham Green, 24 May 1909, with the children from the Metropolitan and City Police Orphanage taking part in the march past. Twickenham High School is in the centre on the far side of the Hampton Road.

Trafalgar Junior School, 1920s. The teacher at the rear of the classroom is Mr Chenery.

Brinsworth House, Staines Road, c. 1914, about three years after the property had been taken over by the Music Hall Benevolent Institution. To the extreme left is the side of Burton House, one of several substantial eighteenth-century houses which stood along this stretch of the Staines Road, each with grounds down to the River Crane.

The Metropolitan and City Police Orphanage, *c.* 1913. This view is from the Stanley Road and, to the left, shows Wellesley House, the oldest part of the orphanage, built in 1852 as T.J. Scale's Academy. The house was much extended in 1882 and later became a self-contained unit with its own swimming pool, cinema, gymnasium, laundry, workshops and other facilities.

Some of the children of the orphanage photographed in the main entrance, early 1900s. The stripes on the boy's arm indicate the police background to the home.

The main entrance to the Wellesley House wing of the orphanage, early 1900s.

The junction of Stanley Road and Hampton Road with Fifth Cross Road to the right, *c.* 1904. The Nelson public house is in the centre.

Warren Farm Lane, early 1900s. This delightfully rural picture shows a wooden bridge with a sluice gate open to allow water to run off from the River Crane. The lane gave access to Warren Farm, which stood in the Lincoln Avenue/Selkirk Road area, from Staines Road via Mill Road.

Hospital Bridge Road: the bridge over the River Crane, 1911. The road was originally named Teddington Road after the Enclosure of 1818; the name Hospital Bridge Road derives from the army encampments, which included a hospital, in the 1680s on Hounslow Heath in the area now occupied by Whitton School.

Blackmore Farm, Wellington Road, 1919. Also known as Blackmoor Farm, the property had been bought by William Poupart Jnr in 1912. At that time he was living at Fernleigh in Belmont Road. He died in 1939 but his wife lived on at Blackmore Farm until her death in 1961. William's father, also William Poupart, owned Marsh Farm and was a prominent figure in local affairs. The building and access road remain today as part of Squire's Garden Centre.

Ex-King Manoel of Portugal skating on Pen Ponds in Richmond Park, January 1912. The king, who was shortly to move to Fulwell Park, can be seen in the centre left of the picture with his mother standing close by. A contemporary report in the *Richmond and Twickenham Times* recorded that 'crowds of skaters thronged Pen Ponds . . . during the frost which was so severe that the ice was four inches thick. King Manoel was seen skating with considerable success.' Less diplomatically, the writer of the postcard bearing this photograph describes the king as 'learning to skate'.

CHAPTER FIVE

WHITTON

Beale's butcher's shop, High Street, c. 1934. Charles Beale is on the left by the delivery van, outside his shop with his staff. After no more than about five years in these premises he moved the business to Whitton Dene.

The northern end of Percy Road, now Whitton High Street, *c.* 1910, showing the cottages that stood on the site of the present Kneller Furnishings building and Iceland freezer shop. The first two houses, Percy Villas, were demolished in 1937; the others were pulled down after the war. In the background the old Nelson public house can be seen; the house now on that site was built in 1936.

Whitton High Street in 1957 with the last remaining cottages which once occupied the whole of the western side of the road. These cottages were pulled down in 1964 to make way for the parade of shops including the Iceland freezer store. Past the cottages is Colton's furniture shop, followed by the old Whitton Library and the London Co-operative Stores.

Nelson Road looking westward from the Nelson, *c.* 1910. On the left-hand side are the Victorian cottages called Wisteria Place, then Alma Cottages, Hope Cottages and Park Terrace. On the right-hand side is the garden of South Lodge, now a block of flats.

The reverse view of Nelson Road to the above, again *c.* 1910, looking towards the Nelson, whose roof line can be seen between the trees. The newly built Victor Villas are on the left, with the Whitton Laundry at the far end of the terrace.

Aerial view of Kneller Hall in 1936. Kneller Hall is named after Sir Godfrey Kneller, who built a house on the site between 1709 and 1711. The present house is the result of rebuilding in the 1840s, when the building was acquired by the government as a teacher training school; this was opened in 1851, but was not a success. It closed in 1856 and the building was reopened in 1857 as the Royal Military School of Music, which it remains to this day. The newly built Kneller Gardens are in the background. In the left foreground is the Duke of Cambridge public house which opened at the same time as the School of Music.

Workmen repairing the front façade of Kneller Hall in the 1920s. The stained-glass window to the chapel can be seen on the first floor; the window has panes commemorating the past commandants of the School of Music.

Ornamental bridge over the lake in the grounds of Kneller Hall, *c.* 1906. A formal garden with a lake was originally laid out by Sir Godfrey Kneller in the early eighteenth century. Around 1800, the then owner Samuel Prime had the gardens redesigned with a more natural look. The bridge leads to an island on which there was a Chinese summer house. The lake was filled in about 1960 and is part of the Kneller Hall sports field.

The Old Manor House, Whitton Dene, *c*. 1930. The site of a house since the early seventeenth century, later residents included General Primrose, Eleanor Verney, and Thomas Hill. In the early nineteenth century it was the farmhouse of William Corfe. It was demolished in 1935 when Old Manor Drive was built.

The dining room of the Old Manor House, *c*. 1930. An old wooden staircase, leading to the first floor, can be seen in the background.

Richards & Oliver's building and decorating business at 8a Hounslow Road in 1935.

Allenson's General Store and Post Office in Kneller Road, *c*, 1895. The first Whitton post office, it was run by James Allenson from 1848 till his death in 1863 and subsequently by his wife, then his daughter, till about 1899. The building was demolished in 1922 and is now the site of a scrapyard.

The eastern end of Nelson Road, 1909. The parade of shops on the right, known as The Market Place, was built in 1907. Pope's Cottages, the whitewashed buildings on the left, were demolished in the 1930s. Beyond the road sign in the background can just be seen the building of the old Whitton School, which was demolished in 1962.

The South Western public house, Whitton Road, *c.* 1935, named after the London and South Western Railway which runs about fifty yards to the north. The road in the centre of the picture is Whitton Dene, which was only just being developed.

CHAPTER SIX

TEDDINGTON

Hughendon House. This building appears on the 1863 OS map of Teddington and is clearly a substantial house. It has had a very chequered history having been a private dwelling, an estate agent's (as in this picture), a picture gallery and is currently a dentist's surgery.

William Haine was a photographer operating from Park Road Studios, 31 Park Road, from about 1908. He produced many fine views of Teddington, several of which appear in this book. His work is easily recognizable by the embossed signature on his postcards.

The Queen public house, on the corner of Broad Street/Queen's Road, was one of the Isleworth Brewery (later Watneys) pubs in the town. The proprietor is shown as A.E. Wells. Strangely, although there are nowhere near as many pubs in the Hampton end of town, this one appears not to have been successful and closed in the 1950s. It has been converted to a launderette and betting shop but the original façade has been maintained.

Teddington Public School, 1950s/1960s. The original building was a school for boys, built in 1832 by public subscription and with Queen Adelaide as patron. By the time of this picture the school also took in girls and infants. It was demolished in 1974 to make way for a new church and the new school was built in Church Road.

The butcher's shop of Sidney H. Easton at 34 Broad Street on the corner with North Lane, *c.* 1926. This shop remained as a butcher's until the early 1990s when it closed, to reopen later as a charity shop.

Garrud Bros Ltd at 45/47 Broad Street, 1950. This was a popular store which covered the full range of household furnishings. The picture shows a line of hopeful shoppers, forming an orderly queue down Elfin Grove, waiting for the doors to open for the sale.

The Causeway, Christmas 1907: an unusual view showing garlands and flags hanging across the street. In the centre there is a trade banner proclaiming the slogan 'Success to Teddington'.

The event of the first tram in Teddington on 2 April 1903. The tram has just come over Teddington Bridge, past what is now Barclays Bank, and is outside Deayton's Stores (now Iceland but closed). At the back of the tram stands Mr Charles Deayton while his wife may be seen looking out of an upper window of the store.

An advertising card from W. Clark & Sons, Removers and Storers of 4 Church Road. Theirs was the first shop in the small parade after the school. The business was still in existence in the 1950s.

The Causeway, south-west side. Taken from Church Road this view is unusual as it shows the school wall on the left and the church wall on the right, both since demolished. The blinds of Deayton's look very impressive, looming over the pavement.

The St Alban's procession on 17 June 1907. This picture was taken in Teddington High Street as the procession is passing the King's Head and the boot shop of Beaney on the left-hand side. Mr Beaney was a devout church-going man and served at the altar for sixty-seven years from 1891 to 1957.

High Street, Teddington, c. 1910. The area on the left-hand side of the picture has not yet been developed, although the tram service, started in 1903, is running.

A little further up High Street, with the cutting into Field Lane just visible on the right. Although the tramlines are laid down, the only transport to be seen is horse drawn. The awning of Stapletons' the butcher's can be clearly seen on the left-hand side.

High Street, Teddington showing the premises of Frank Hayward, chemist and Stapleton & Sons, butcher's. Stapletons' had taken over the previous butcher's of Ives & Son and this picture shows it in the last years of its existence as a shop. It was acquired by Franco Llangella and carefully renovated, keeping many of the original features. It then reopened as Shambles wine bar.

This could be called 'Road Meets Rail' and was during the mid-1950s when the 27 bus from Highgate used to terminate in Adelaide Road. The buses would then proceed into Victoria Road, turn into Albert Road and then right into Park Road for the return trip. Something went slightly wrong on this day and the bus mounted the kerb and collided with the station canopy above the entrance.

The Railway Hotel was established in the 1860s, after the coming of the railway to Teddington. The landlord at this time was J. Braid. This picture shows a small crowd gathering outside as if waiting for the doors to open – unless they obligingly came out for the camera. This is a typical Victorian backstreet pub of the period.

The Tudor Court Hotel stood in Park Road almost opposite the Adelaide. Despite the style of the building, it was not very old. It does not appear to have been a very successful venture and no entries appear in any local directories of the day. In its last years, it gained a seedy reputation as the haunt of some unsavoury characters. It was pulled down in the mid-1970s and a block of flats – Tudor Court – now stands in its place.

Taken in 1935/6, this picture shows Avril Lansdell, with her mother Elsie and baby brother Ray in the pram, walking along Broad Street. They were accosted by photographer F. Stockwell of 45 Broad Street on a promotional mission, hence the mother's severe look.

Shops at Teddington Bridge, late 1940s/early 1950s. The Mikado Tea Rooms later became an antiques shop; the Bridge Toy Shop, run by two sisters – the Misses Watson – was where a good deal of my pocket money ended up; the others are an electrical retailer's and a launderette.

A sign of the post-war political recovery in the local parties. This picture shows a recruitment drive by the Teddington Young Conservatives along Waldegrave Road in 1948.

Teddington Library. This picture shows the second library for Teddington; the first had been in Broad Street where Fuller's off-licence now stands. This building is in Waldegrave Road, was designed by Henry Cheers and opened in 1906 with a bequest from Andrew Carnegie of £4,857. One of the doors of the adjacent fire station can be seen on the right-hand side of this picture.

A picture taken by William Haine of the Revd Francis Leith Boyd and the altar servers of St Alban's. The four processional banners in the background suggest that this may have been taken before the annual St Alban's day procession which was held on the saint's feast day.

Linden Grove, seen here at around the turn of the century, is a small row of houses between Waldegrave Road and the railway track. There used to be a level crossing here until the 1960s when it was replaced by a pedestrian foot bridge.

A mystery photograph – Udney Park Garage. Despite claiming to have been established in 1920, it does not seem to have done a very good job of advertising itself as local directories do not carry any entries for it. The TED. Lock telephone number would indicate a date of about 1955 when Teddington first had its own telephone exchange and the MOLesey prefix was discontinued.

Whoever the Diamond Bonus Co. were, they certainly had an impressive fleet of vehicles, operating from Diamond House which was next to Central Garage in Waldegrave Road. The company was owned by George W. Blackwell but beyond this, nothing more is known. The reverse of this card contains a printed message to say that some goods have been dispatched by car.

Teddington Swimming Baths was opened in Vicarage Road in 1931 by the Teddington Urban District Council. Like most of the swimming baths of the time, it was open-air and not enclosed until many years later. Note the water chute in the far corner.

The workshops of Normansfield Hospital, a part of the hospital complex founded by Dr John Langdon-Down in 1868. This far-seeing man established a community within the hospital with a working farm and workshops where some of the patients produced a range of goods for resale. The workshops are still standing, still in use and are listed, which is perhaps as well, in view of the uncertainty surrounding the future of Normansfield.

Miss Katie Blackmore RBA was a popular artist who exhibited widely between 1913 and 1939. She moved around London and the Home Counties, having two stays in Hampton Wick and one in Teddington. Her principle works are 'The Mushroom Dance' and 'The Enchanted Pool'.

The Lensbury Club, photographed on 24 October 1957. Built and opened in 1938 as the Sports and Social Club for the employees of the Shell Petroleum Company, it has been subsequently altered and extended and now operates as a conference centre, though there is currently some doubt as to its future.

The caption on this photograph is 'Hospital Fête Teddington 1923'. The Teddington and Hampton Wick Cottage Hospital had opened in 1875 in Elfin Grove with a capacity for six patients. As may be imagined, it did not take long before more capacity was required and a new hospital, built by public subscription, opened in 1929. Perhaps this shows the fund-raising committee and staff.

Celebrations in Gomer Gardens for the coronation of Edward VII, 1902. Edward had been a popular Prince of Wales and when the time came for him to take the throne, the population gave him its full support. Scenes such as this were common across the country.

A shot of the Teddington Trades Exhibition of 1907. This was an amazingly successful venture, held in the grounds of the Clarence Hotel. It was opened by Mrs Langdon-Down who was accompanied by her son, Dr Percival Langdon-Down JP. Nearly every business in the town was represented, all stands being under canvas and this picture shows the stall of W. Humphrey.

The Council School, April 1907; almost certainly the Stanley Road school which was the first built by and operated by the Local Authority. The way in which the desks are tiered is typical of the method of council administration at that time, to improve supervision of the pupils. The angelic-faced boy, second from the right, is Will Chapman.

The character on the horse rejoiced in the nickname of 'Mother's Pretty Boy' but by all accounts was anything but. He ran a fruit and vegetable stall in Stanley Road and was well known for his abrasive tongue in dealing with not only his customers but anyone who had the misfortune to cross his patch.

The Pavement Grocery Stores. A typical shop scene with the proprietor, complete with long white apron, standing in the doorway. The Pavement was a row of shops off the Kingston Road in Bushy Park Road. The advertising signs in the window reflect the tastes of the day with cocoa being the most popular drink.

The Grove Teddington or Teddington Grove was built *c*. 1760 for Moses Franks, a wealthy Jewish merchant who died in Teddington in 1789. It later belonged to John Walter, the founder of *The Times*, who died in 1812. The house was subsequently used as the scene of several hospital fund-raising activities. This picture was taken by William Haine and was probably one of the last taken of the house as it was demolished shortly after the First World War.

Teddington Pond. The old village pond stood roughly where the railway track runs under the road bridge today. It was drained and filled in as the railway was laid in the early 1860s. At this time, there was massive sand and gravel extraction from land adjoining the railway off Sandy Lane and from the crater that was left, this new pond was created. At least one sailing club operated here and this picture shows a fisherman in his boat with rod in hand. The pond continued until the time of the Second World War when it was drained and later filled with rubble from the blitz of London's East End. After a suitable period of settlement, the estates of Shaef Way and Harrowdene Gardens were built on the site.

The Savoy cinema replaced an earlier picture house, the Elmfield, which had been built by Elijah Landen in 1900. The film showing is 'Turkey Time' starring Bing Crosby. This building was pulled down in 1937 and a bigger and better Savoy was rebuilt in its place with a capacity of over 1,500.

The fine gentlemen in this photo look to be members of a cycling club. The photograph was taken by Herbert Salmon of The Causeway and he operated there between 1896 and 1898. The grand doorway at the rear on the right-hand side certainly suggests a house of some importance.

The High Street, showing No. 124, the premises of Alfred Gardner, which opened in 1927 and continued trading successfully up to the end of the Second World War. Mr Gardner and his family in fact lived at 173 Waldegrave Road. The shop is still a grocer's today.

Cart from W. Poupart & Sons of Twickenham, Teddington and Hampton. Poupart's had premises in all three towns and in Teddington operated from Marsh Farm Dairy (now Yogi's) in the High Street.

CHAPTER SEVEN

RIVERSIDE

The Gardens, Teddington Lock. The first lock was built at Teddington in 1811 and consisted very much of the launch lock that we know today. The barge lock was then cut through the mainland in 1904, creating a lock island between the two. The lock keeper's offices on the island were rather spartan and, not surprisingly, the keepers made good use of their spare time to brighten their environment and thus created the lock gardens.

The paddle steamer SS *Queen Elizabeth* going through the barge lock at Teddington Lock. Pleasure craft of this type were very popular with Londoners until the Second World War, after which cars gradually became more affordable. In this picture the bridge over the lock cut can be seen in the distance. This steamer sank off Kew Pier on 5 September 1904.

Teddington Weir with the eastern end of the lock island. A fish weir was first established here in 1345 when the Manor of Teddington was governed by Westminster Abbey. A weir has been maintained ever since and became more important after the lock cut was made. The present weir was built in 1812 and has been substantially renovated since, particularly in 1995/6.

The skiff lock was added to Teddington Lock at the time of its first major rebuild in 1858 and a boatslide was added to the lock rollers in 1869 to facilitate the progress of small craft without having to open the lock. As this picture was taken during the Victorian golden age of boating, this must have proved to be a very convenient addition to the lock for a swift passage for small pleasure boats.

A general view of the locks, with the lock rollers on the left. The menacing guillotine sluice separates the skiff lock from the launch lock and the barge lock is on the extreme right.

Another view of Teddington Weir, showing a fishing punt in quiet waters.

A typical view of boating in the Teddington backwater around Trowlock Island. The scene shows many young ladies sitting upright in skiffs while their beaux took to the oars and rowed them along the river.

CHAPTER EIGHT

HAMPTON WICK

Hampton Wick from the air. This picture shows part of Bushy Park on the left-hand side foreground and the centre of Hampton Wick town. The scene is dominated by the gasometers of the Hampton Court Gas Company which later became part of British Gas. The last of the gasometers was demolished in 1994.

Clennon, St. John's Road, Hampton Wick.

Clennon, St John's Road, Hampton Wick. It is not clear whether the name Clennon refers to the name of a house or to the elegantly dressed gentleman who looks as if he is about to burst into song. Any information about this picture would be very much appreciated.

High Street, Hampton Wick. A range of buildings that would have been demolished in 1902 to make way for the trams. The disruption that this caused is hard to imagine but almost one complete side of the High Street had to be taken down to allow for two parallel sets of tramlines to be laid.

C.J. Winterbourne, grocer's in Hampton Wick High Street, *c.* 1890. This was a successful business which expanded into the double shopfront we see here. The business was acquired later by R.J. Belchamber and continued as a successful shop until the Second World War. The buildings are still standing, although slightly altered, today.

High Street, Hampton Wick. The buildings in the picture are empty and boarded up, awaiting demolition. They were pulled down in 1902 as part of a road-widening programme, following agreement to introduce the London United Tramway service.

Lower Teddington Road, Hampton Wick, *c.* 1910. This road is a continuation of Broom Road from Teddington, after it has crossed the parish boundary, to run to the junction of Hampton Wick by the Swan public house. This view looks towards Teddington.

This picture shows a crowd watching the laying of the foundation stone of the Roynayne Hall in Church Grove on 25 June 1927. Standing in a checked suit with her side to the camera and performing the opening ceremony is HRH The Princess Royal, Countess of Harewood.

Willow Camp and Tea Gardens, Hampton Wick. This site is now the Aries Sailing Club (BBC sailing Club) and is slightly upstream of the Tamesis Club. I am indebted to Mr W. Manning of Sunbury for identifying the exact location.

Teddington Reach. An unusual view of the River Thames from the Teddington bank showing the elm tree and Ham Fields on the left and some of the large houses on the towpath.

The well-loaded pleasure vessel *Sunbury Belle* seen here at Kingston Wharf. On the opposite side of the river is Burgoine's Boatyard which operated until 1985.

CHAPTER NINE

BUSHY PARK

The first pavilion of Teddington Cricket and Hockey Club in Bushy Park. The Cricket Club lost its original green in the centre of the town, when the railway came in 1863, and then moved into Bushy Park. Teddington Hockey Club was born out of the Cricket Club in 1871 and used the same site. The two clubs combined their efforts to construct this pavilion which opened in 1893.

Some of the devastation in Bushy Park following the hurricane on 1 June 1908. This picture was taken by the popular Teddington firm of Young & Co. and shows a fallen tree lying across the drinking fountain.

Another picture, taken by William Haine, showing a fallen tree having been blown on to a perimeter wall between the park and Sandy Lane. The workers in the foreground are lopping branches off and clearing these to open the road again.

After the First World War, King George V granted Upper Lodge to the London County Council as an open-air school for boys from London's East End and it became known as the King's Canadian School. This picture shows the building of Upper Lodge itself.

'The Paddling Stream' at the King's Canadian School. There were some extensive water gardens at Upper Lodge, which had been laid out by the Earl of Halifax, and several of these water features were utilized by the school.

Part of the Woodland Gardens; this picture is entitled 'The Bird Sanctuary'. These gardens were created by the park authorities and opened to the public in 1925. They were actually made as a result of a government scheme to assist the unemployed by using their labour to transform the parkland.

Another view of the Woodland Gardens, this time showing the lily pond.

CHAPTER TEN

HAMPTON

Aerial view of Hampton, 1929. This view was part of the aerial survey of Hampton, undertaken by the UDC in 1929. On the extreme right the white building by the river, in front of Garrick's Villa, is Temple House. Temple House only existed from 1923 to 1932: there was such an outcry over a building being joined on to Garrick's Temple that it was purchased by the UDC and the land turned into the public open space, Garrick's Lawn. The view also shows the tiny sailing club island before the sailing club was built. The overall view is of a recognizable but less hectic environment, the lack of traffic being particularly noticeable.

Aerial view of the Karsino, Tagg's Island, *c.* 1930. The domed, circular building is the Palm Court Theatre also used as a concert pavilion and ballroom. The building was 100 feet by 90 feet wide with a seating capacity of over 600 and a magnificent maple floor for dancing. On the right-hand side are some of the many tennis courts that then existed. The island was reached by vehicle ferry from the Middlesex (left) side or by passenger ferry from the Surrey (right) side. In 1940 A.C. Cars moved to the island and the first bridge was built; the present bridge replaced it in 1982. In 1983 the centre of the island was excavated to create a lagoon for mooring houseboats.

Vehicle ferry to the Thames Riviera, Tagg's Island, *c.* 1930. The hotel and leisure complex on Tagg's Island, formerly the Karsino which had opened in 1913 and run by Fred Karno, was reopened as the Thames Riviera in 1928 under new ownership. This picture shows the steam-powered vehicle ferry, with smoke coming from its chimney, which ran between the island and the Middlesex bank. There was a garage which could accommodate forty cars on the island. There was also a foot ferry to the Surrey bank. New facilities at the Thames Riviera included a covered tennis court with artificial sunlight and a skating rink with artificial ice, both very advanced facilities in 1928.

Henry Ripley, standing outside Feathers Cottage in Thames Street, *c.* 1885. Henry Ripley was Hampton's first local historian, who published *The History and Topography of Hampton on Thames* in 1884. It was the first history of Hampton and formed the groundwork and basis for much that has been published since on Hampton. Henry, with his son Everard Henry Ripley (in the doorway), then lived in Feathers Cottage, now coincidently owned by one of the co-authors of this book, and Garrick Cottage, on the right. Henry was headmaster at the English School as well as organist and choirmaster at St Mary's Church; he died in 1902.

Unloading a sailing barge at Bell Hill, *c.* 1900. This particular barge is unloading bricks into 'tumbrels' which were horse-drawn tip-carts of one-ton capacity. These sailing barges also carried coal, cement, timber and other goods and had a crew of one man and a boy. In the background Hurst Park Racecourse and Grandstand can be seen. Bell Hill recreation ground was laid out in 1884. In 1910 a formal landing stage was constructed at the foot of Bell Hill, replacing the 'shore' that then existed, at a cost of £370.

The head of Garrick's Ait with St Mary's Church in the background, *c.* 1925. The island was, as the name implies, part of the Garrick estate at one time. Around this time the island was used for mooring, camping or picnicking for which charges were made. Later tents or canvas-covered, wooden-framed seasonal bungalows appeared, before the modern-day bungalows. St Mary's Church, seen here with Bell Hill recreation ground in front, was built in 1831. It replaced an earlier medieval church, demolished in 1829, whose capacity had been outgrown.

Hurst Park Races on a Bank Holiday, *c.* 1900. Huge numbers of racegoers used the ferry from Hampton across to Molesey. Molesey Hurst was the venue for the old Hampton races until 1887. In 1889 the Hurst Park Club was formed, using the same location. In 1913 suffragettes set fire to, and destroyed, the royal box and the greater part of the grandstand. Racing continued at Hurst Park until the 1960s.

Hampton ferry and ferry boat shed, *c.* 1955. On the island, occupied by the sailing club, is moored *King Edward*. The club was founded in 1944 by twenty-eight people and *King Edward* acted as a club house from 1951 to 1962. The present sailing club building was constructed in 1962 and has been extended since. The lease to Benn's Island was acquired in 1945 from the Thames Conservancy. The ferry is one of the oldest on the Thames, having operated since at least 1519. The ferry boat shed later burnt down and the present building was constructed in 1981. The revitalized ferry was reopened in 1996 under new ownership, with a motorized ferry and now offers boat hire as in former days.

Hampton Fire Brigade, Church Parade, *c.* 1910. This view looking up High Street from the junction with Thames Street shows one of the church parades taking place. These parades were often used for charitable fund-raising and were great events. The processions sometimes consisted of forty or fifty fire appliances from neighbouring brigades as well as different marching bands.

A view looking up High Street, from the junction with Thames Street, c. 1905. On the right-hand side can be seen the sign for the Jolly Gardeners and beyond, on a beam overhanging the road, the sign for the Jolly Coopers. The Jolly Coopers is now the oldest pub in Hampton still occupying the original premises (many others have been rebuilt on their sites or turned to other uses). The building on the extreme left is that of G. Kingsbury & Son Ltd before the Station Road premises were acquired. The large building on the left with the pantile roof was rebuilt in 1908 and was Barclays Bank for many years.

The Jolly Gardeners, with Thomas Bridgeman, the landlord, c. 1890. The Jolly Gardeners was sold to Ashby's of Staines, Brewers and Bankers, in 1890 for £1,500. Ashby's bank was taken over by Barclays in 1903 and its former Hampton sub-branch rebuilt opposite the Jolly Gardeners. The Jolly Gardeners was taken over by Charles Peter Heath in 1936 and the pub closed in 1955. The premises were then used by C.P. Heath the boat-builder. The business, continued by Peter Heath (son of Charles) and John Heath (son of Peter) still operates from the property.

Thames Street looking west, *c.* 1955. On the extreme right is the side entrance to the Red Lion, with the Tudor Restaurant beside it. Although Thames Street, the former shopping centre of Hampton before the arrival of the motor car, was long past its heyday many shops still remained at this time. At present the second-hand bookshop, run by Ian Sheridan, is the sole remaining retail shop left in Thames Street which was once lined with shops and pubs. The Red Lion, rebuilt in 1908 partly to widen Thames Street at the junction with High Street, ceased to be a pub around 1980 and is now used as offices by Geoff Howe and Associates.

Thames Street, looking west, *c.* 1880. The Candle Works, with its triangular pediment, has recently (1997) provided a site for a new building with a similar triangular roof line with a circular decoration! The building with a shop projecting into the road, on the right-hand side, was demolished and replaced by the fire station which opened in 1898 and which now houses a commercial photography business. The building in the centre distance is Jessamine House, demolished in 1957, with the site now used as a display area for vehicles belonging to G. Kingsbury & Son Ltd.

Jessamine House, Thames Street, *c.* 1956. Jessamine House was believed to have been built in 1771 for Thomas Rosoman, founder of Sadler's Wells, and remained in the hands of his family until 1870. Thereafter it was used as an overflow school for the Latin School, nowadays Hampton School, until the new school was built on the Upper Sunbury Road in 1880. George Jenner Kingsbury lived in the house after Kingsbury's acquired the house in the 1920s, until the Second World War when it was loaned to the National Fire Service. Its condition deteriorated, being used as flats after the war and it was demolished in 1957. The site is now used as a display area for cars by Kingsbury's Garage.

The Metropolitan Water Board Fire Brigade, *c.* 1910. In addition to the Hampton Volunteer Fire Brigade the water companies had their own fire brigade. Previously known as the Southwark & Vauxhall Brigade this became the Metropolitan Water Board Brigade in 1903. There was always great competition between the volunteers' and the water companies' brigades to arrive first at a fire. As the two brigades were both based in Thames Street, on opposite sides of the road, this sometimes resulted in near collision in their haste to get out ahead of each other.

Hampton Co-operative Stores, Station Road, 2 March 1907: Delegates Conference. Apart from the two staff in the shop door there are twenty-six people (presumably all delegates) standing by the shop. The Hampton and New Hampton Co-operative Society sold clothing, visible in the right-hand shop, as well as provisions in the left-hand shop. The society had started in a small room in Milton Road in 1879 and soon was able to open the Station Road shop. In latter days the left-hand shop housed the Co-op butcher's. The Co-op finally closed around 1979, just about a century after its humble beginnings. The premises are now occupied by Not Just Tiles.

Looking down Station Road, c. 1905. The World's End is on the extreme left and the photographer is standing close to the corner of Belgrade Road. The trees, today very large, had been newly planted in the 1890s by the council. The view is obviously posed as the children are all looking directly at the camera. Not a single car is visible in Station Road!

Station Road at the junction with Warfield Road (left) and Belgrade Road (right), *c.* 1913. At this time the pillar box was on the Belgrade Road corner, but it is now located across the road on the Warfield Road corner. The first shop on the left-hand side is Tickner, Decorators and next door is A.K. Shaw, Grocery & Provisions. The building with the single-storey addition at the front is the World's End. The addition was built in 1901, presumably after a change of ownership as the previous proprietor had died in 1900. The two shops on the left have now been rebuilt and are presently occupied by a dry-cleaner's and a grocer's/wine merchant's shop.

A close-up of A.K. Shaw, Grocery & Provisions at 92 Station Road. (See previous picture for exact location of shop, now rebuilt.) Goods advertised in the window include tea at 1*s* 4*d*, self-raising flour at 2½*d* per bag and boxes of flake tapioca and flake rice for 1*d*. Peek Frean biscuits and Quaker Oats can also be seen in the window. Fruit and vegetables displayed outside include Spanish onions at 1*d* a bag (7 lb for 6*d*), King Edward potatoes 3 lb for 2*d*, and apples at 2*d* per lb.

The May Queen, *c.* 1925. The picture was taken at the end of Warfield Road. The girl with the long hair who was the May Queen is Mrs Walby (née Helena Heavens). She still lives in the road and has done so all her life (except for three years in the war when the family were bombed out and were temporarily in Tudor Road). Mrs Walby's father, William Heavens (below), was a Hampton policeman and bought the house when it was new in 1903.

A studio portrait of William Heavens, taken early in the century.

The Railway Inn, Station Road, *c.* 1960. This pub, now demolished, stood where Station Close is now situated. The curved wall, the lower courses of which still exist, on the left-hand side of the picture identifies the exact location. Confusingly, The Railway Inn, The Railway Bell and The Railway public houses (the latter two still existing) were all located within 200 yards of each other.

Station Road filter beds under construction in 1902. The filter beds, which were demolished and filled in for a housing development in 1997, are shown here under construction. The site was formerly occupied by Hill House, a large mansion which was demolished in 1901. During construction of the filter beds a temporary tramway was laid in Station Road to transport the excavated material. The spoil was dumped on the land behind the Scout Hut, now used as a football field, and accounts for the field being considerably higher than the surrounding land.

View towards Hampton Station, on extreme left, *c.* 1920. The building with the ornate roof on the right is the Jubilee Almshouses, built to celebrate Queen Victoria's Golden Jubilee in 1887 although there was a 'final appeal' in the Diamond Jubilee year of 1897 to raise the remaining money for their construction. Prior to the building of the almshouses there stood nearby a row of six single-storey almshouses built in 1723. Nowadays the Jubilee Almshouses have themselves been replaced by Jubilee House, in which the elderly are still cared for.

Beards Hill, shortly after construction in 1903. The houses shown here, as well as some in Oldfield Road and Rose Hill, were constructed as 'workmen's cottages' by the Urban District Council. Hampton UDC purchased Rose Hill, the former home of John Beard, a famous eighteenth-century actor and singer, in 1902. The house 'Rose Hill' was used to provide offices for the council and also a free library. The offices were no longer required after the amalgamation with Teddington and Twickenham in 1937, but the library remains. Much of the land was used to construct fifty-six workmen's cottages and was some of the earliest council housing in the country.

Oldfield Road near the junction with Percy Road, looking towards Beards Hill and Rose Hill, *c*. 1930. The curved sign above the fence on the right-hand side says 'M.W.B. Hampton Employees' Club and Institute'. This corrugated iron building, still existing on the site and now used for industrial purposes has had many uses. In the 1890s it housed a navvies' Mission, for labourers and others working on the extension to the waterworks; it was briefly placed in the Upper Sunbury Road and then moved to Station Road. While there it was used temporarily as an overflow boys' school until Percy Road School was completed in 1907. The building was then sold for £100 and moved to the corner of Oldfield Road where it became premises for a social club for water board employees.

Milton Road, Hampton, *c*. 1930. The total lack of cars is the most obvious clue to the age of the picture. Many of the houses in Milton Road date from the 1880s and even earlier. There was a further spate of building in the last three years of the nineteenth century. Plans for eighteen cottages were approved in 1897 and 1898. Among those built at that time were the terraces at the south end of the road, Essex Villas and Easter Terrace.

Newport's shop at the Triangle, *c.* 1920. The shop sold fruit, confectionery, drinks and other provisions, and had some splendid advertising signs on the shopfront. Two pairs of tramlines can be seen in Church Street. The old clapboard house to the left of Newport's was demolished in about 1929. The shop, for many years known as The Pantry, finally closed in the 1990s and was converted into a house in 1996.

Charabanc outing from the White Hart, *c.* 1930. The charabanc was widely used before the advent of the motor coach for group outings. For many the trip might be the only day out of the year. The present building shown in the picture was constructed in 1901, replacing an earlier eighteenth-century one which had formerly been known as the Six Bells, named after the six bells installed in 1679 at the old St Mary's Church. At one time David Garrick, the famous eighteenth-century Shakespearean actor, owned the property.

White Hart Cottages, beside the White Hart, 1961. These cottages were demolished shortly after this photo was taken, although their location can be determined by reference to the cellar doors to the White Hart, in the ground on the extreme left, which still remain. The view can be dated exactly due to the construction of King's Paddock where careful examination of the photo shows scaffolding on the building under construction, behind the van.

Douai House on the right, with No. 98 High Street and Drake Cottage on the left. Douai House stood on what is now the entrance to Douai Grove. Its exact location can be determined by reference to the adjoining cottages pictured here which still stand.

The Drill Hall, *c.* 1960. This building, next to the Duke's Head, was built in 1805, by public subscription, as a School of Industry for girls. It was the first girls' school in Hampton and taught reading, writing and needlework. The building did not meet the requirements of the 1870 Education Act and became the premises of a Working Men's Club. Then it was used as a drill hall and headquarters of G Company of the 2nd Volunteer Battalion, Middlesex Regiment. Later it became a motorworks, as shown here, and was demolished in the 1960s. A petrol station was built on the site, now converted to an MOT testing station. The cottage on the left-hand side still stands.

Festivities at the laying of the memorial stone at the All Saints' Church, Hampton, on 13 June 1908. The stone was laid by HRH Princess Christian of Schleswig-Holstein. The church was already partly erected 'being up to a height sufficient to receive a roof'. It was consecrated by the Bishop of London in November 1908. The original design incorporated a tower, although in the event this was not built.

Bernard Garside, Hampton local historian, in November 1962. This picture, taken by Stan March, shows Bernard Garside standing beside one of the large boundary oak trees in Broad Lane, shortly before his death the following year, at the age of sixty-four. Bernard Garside was a prolific local historian who wrote, and published, a series of ten books on various aspects of Hampton in the sixteenth and seventeenth centuries (published between 1937 and 1958). In addition he wrote the history of Hampton School, first published in 1931, and a brief history of the school for their 400th anniversary in 1957.

Beating the bounds, Hampton, 1893. Generally every seven years on Ascension Day the centuries-old practice of 'beating the bounds' – perambulating the parish boundaries – took place. However, after the 1893 ceremony depicted here, for some reason the next occasion took place only five years later in 1898. The final full ceremony took place in 1905 although there was a smaller-scale event eight years later in 1913 on 18 June.

CHAPTER ELEVEN

HAMPTON HILL

View from St James's spire, c. 1903. This view is looking south-east, as under a magnifying glass the tallest building (just left of centre) can be seen to be what is now the United Reformed Church, which is south-east of St James's Church. The view is before St James's Avenue was built on the fields in the foreground of the picture.

New Pantile Bridge under construction in 1910. Although the trams had first come to the area in 1903, much of the line in Hampton Hill High Street was initially single-track with passing loops. Road widening, which required the demolition of numerous buildings, was a protracted affair, starting in 1904 but not reaching the point shown above, which necessitated a new bridge, until 1910. The previous bridge, built in 1832 was a narrow bridge with a watersplash beside it through which the heavy traffic had to pass.

Civil Defence Corps, Pantile Bridge, Hampton Hill. This view shows a Civil Defence Corps inspection by Mayor Beckett.

Hampton Volunteer Fire Brigade outside its fire station in Hampton Hill High Street, *c.* 1900. The Hampton Hill volunteers had been set up in 1876 and subsequently amalgamated with the Hampton volunteers. The Hampton Hill Fire Station was constructed in 1898/9 and was opened in October 1899. The building, however, had a remarkably short life, being demolished in August 1904. This was due to the need to widen the High Street to accommodate double tram tracks and £955 compensation was received from London United Tramways. The new fire station (now part of the library) was opened in April 1906 in Windmill Road.

High Street, Hampton Hill, near junction with Holly Road, *c.* 1905. The advertising hoardings on the left locate the former position of the fire station and other buildings demolished in 1904 for road widening for the trams. The building on the near side of Holly Road was then offering haircutting and shampooing and is now occupied by John Hodgson's World of Lighting. On the far side of Holly Road are the premises then occupied by J.C. Allen that now house Hampton Hill Antiques.

High Street, Hampton Hill, near the junction with Park Place, *c.* 1910. The Congregational Church (now the United Reformed Church) can be seen with its miniature spire, which is now gone. The church opened in 1870 and before that, services had been held in Windmill Road in what later became the Spiritualist Church. The view, apart from the tramlines, is very similar today. The corner shop occupying the premises to the left of the church is Threshers Wine Shop nowadays.

Looking south along High Street, Hampton Hill, *c.* 1925. Most old views of the High Street look north so this view is unusual. On the right-hand side the corner sign of the new Crown and Anchor (rebuilt in 1907 due to road widening for the trams), at the junction with Windmill Road, can be seen. The Crown and Anchor subsequently became the Valiant Knight and is now Joe's Restaurant. On the extreme left is the Morden Dairy and on a signboard a couple of shops down can be seen the sign of Hampton Hill Post Office. The post office continued in this building until 1995 and then moved northwards along the High Street.

The Longford River alongside Windmill Road, c. 1910. The Longford River has previously been known as the Cardinals River, as well as the King's, Queen's, Wolsey's and the New River. It is in fact a man-made canal 11 miles long and 21 feet wide, built to supply Hampton Court and its fountains with water, and was excavated by order of King Charles I in 1638/9. The building in the centre is the Windmill pub, rebuilt in 1901. The previous public house was constructed on the same site in 1868, across the river from the actual windmill. The windmill itself was built in 1785 and demolished in 1876.

Eastbank Road looking towards the junction with Cross Street, c. 1905. This very unusual early picture of a minor side street shows a view which is little changed to this day. At a meeting of the Urban District Council in 1897 the surveyor was instructed to prepare plans for the making-up (surfacing) of a number of roads, including Eastbank Road. There were delays due to the difficulty of obtaining a loan to cover the cost of the development, and also due to the inefficiency of the contractor. The work was finally completed in 1899.

High Street looking towards the Park Terrace shops, c. 1955. The trolleybus wires can be seen overhead (the last trolleybuses ran in 1962). In the centre of the picture a signboard for Stanley's Bakeries can be seen (in the premises now occupied by the Cavan Bakeries). Visible with the aid of a magnifying glass is the fact that A. Boyall, General Builders and Ironmongers then occupied the premises on the other side of the Park Road junction – now occupied by the Hampton Hill Framing Company.

High Street, Hampton Hill, c. 1925. This view shows the junction of High Street looking westwards up Park Road. The large building is that of Jones & Peers, now occupied by the Hampton Hill Framing Company and Hampton Hill Gallery. The sign across the road refers to a fund-raising fête for the new Teddington Hospital; many such events were held in the 1920s. The new hospital opened in 1929.

View looking towards Hampton Road, *c.* 1905. This picture, taken from the end of Park Road near the junction with High Street, looks eastwards down Hampton Road. The premises on the extreme left were those of Jones & Peers, who advertised themselves as Water and Sanitary Engineers, Furnishing and General Ironmongers as well as complete house furnishers and also able to undertake house decorations. The building on the left on the corner with the High Street was then Matthews Stores, nowadays known as Ashton House. It is interesting to note that on the corner of the building a sign saying 'Matthews Stores 1895' still exists.

Burton's Road, Hampton Hill, *c.* 1909. A snowy winter's day in Burton's Road from the edge of the railway bridge. The brick wall on the right-hand side is the edge of the railway bridge and the view looks down Burton's Road towards the High Street. The houses on the right-hand side are easily recognizable today, although the land on the left-hand side has been built over. Burton's Road is a very old road, possibly a seventeenth-century track, which served as a dividing line between what was then part of Hounslow Heath and Hampton Common.

Interior of St James's Church, *c.* 1905. The church, consecrated in December 1863, was built on the then existing common or glebe land belonging to St Mary's Church, Hampton. It was a simple structure when first built, consisting of nave, chancel and vestry room. By 1876 the north and south aisles, porch and organ chamber had all been added and the chancel had been enlarged. The tower and spire were added in 1887 to celebrate Queen Victoria's Golden Jubilee. Most of this work was inspired by the Revd Fitzroy John Fitzwygram, the first vicar, who spent most of his private fortune on building up the infrastructure and housing for the village. He died in 1881.

Queen's Road under a heavy fall of snow in 1938. This view, taken on Boxing Day 1938, shows a good number of inches of snow. We can assume that the photographer lived at 11a Queen's Road, as another picture was taken on Christmas Eve of that year from a bedroom window at that address. It seems that the snow lasted for several days and that possibly fresh snow had also fallen, judging by the untouched nature of what we can see in the photograph.

CHAPTER TWELVE

HAMPTON COURT

The Cardinal Wolsey Hotel, Hampton Court Road, c. 1910. An obviously posed publicity picture which seems to include all the staff. There are some splendid early vending machines on the side wall of the hotel. The Cardinal Wolsey stands on the site of an old barn which was there in the mid-seventeenth century. Later, in a different building, another pub called Ye Chequers stood on the site of the present-day Cardinal Wolsey.

Bank Holiday crowds at Hampton Court Fair in 1913 or 1914. Fairs have long been held on Hampton Court Green, probably regularly, for more than a century. In January 1913 HM Office of Works advertised in the *Surrey Comet* for tenders for the privilege of erecting stalls, swings, etc. on Hampton Court Green on Bank Holidays that year. Large crowds have long been attracted to the fairs and the *Surrey Comet* recorded in 1909 complaints of the state of Hampton Court Green after Bank Holidays. The tramways were then asked to provide boxes on the tramcars for all the used tickets.

The Cook House, Hampton Court House in autumn 1914. Hampton Court House, a very large house behind Hampton Court Green, was built in 1757. It was at the heart of social affairs in Hampton until the De Wette family left in 1903. It did not sell at auction in 1903, 1905 and 1910 but was sold in 1912 to a purchaser who did not occupy it and was obviously being used by the army in this picture postcard (posted in October 1914). Later the house was owned by the Gore-Lloyd family until sold to the Middlesex County Council in 1945. At the time of publication the owner, Richmond Council, has the property up for sale.

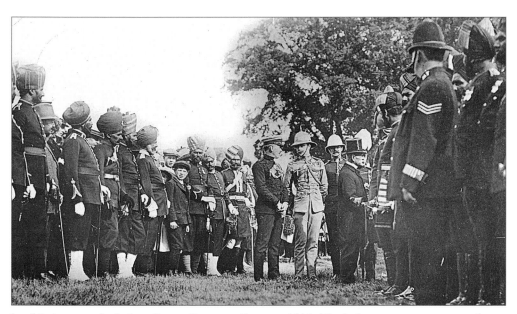

Lord Roberts at the Indian Camp, Hampton Court in 1911. The Indian troops were camped near Hampton Court as a domicile for their participation in the coronation of George V in June 1911. Indian troops had also camped in the area for the coronation of Edward VII in 1902. Lord Roberts was educated at Hill House School in Hampton. Hill House was demolished in 1901 to make way for the Station Road filter beds. The filter beds were themselves demolished and filled in during 1997 to make way for the Hampton Green housing development.

The tram terminus at Hampton Court, c. 1905. Electric trams came to Hampton Court in 1903, when there were two routes forming a loop. One route came from Stanley Road via Teddington and Hampton Wick to Hampton Court (and from Stanley Road connected to Richmond Bridge). The other also came from the junction at Stanley Road (where it connected to a track to Shepherd's Bush) and went in a loop via Hampton Hill and Hampton down to Hampton Court. In the early days the trams were open-top, as shown here, but later roofed tramcars were used.

Mitre Hotel, Hampton Court, *c.* 1905. The old brick toll house can be seen on the left-hand side of the picture. Tolls ceased in 1876 and nowadays the toll house is incorporated as part of the Mitre Hotel. In the seventeenth century the Mitre, in an earlier building, stood on the site beside the then existing ferry which closed after the first Hampton Court Bridge opened in 1753. It is thought that the name Mitre may refer to the sharp twists and turns in the road in the vicinity.

An aerial view of Hampton Court Palace, *c.* 1925. This view clearly shows the older Tudor portion of the palace, including the main entrance in the west front. This part of the palace was mainly built by Cardinal Wolsey and Henry VIII in the 1520s and 1530s. The later portion at the back was built by Wren for William and Mary in the period 1689–1700. The 'new' Wren king's and queen's apartments replaced much of Henry's work, including the king's and queen's lodgings.

The Trophy Gates, Hampton Court Palace, *c.* 1910. The main entrance (west front) is reached through the Trophy Gates, built in the reign of William III (1689–1702), and altered by George II (who reigned 1727–60). The outer gate pillars are surmounted by lead trophies of arms. The inner gate pillars have a lion on one and a unicorn on the other (both supporting shields with the arms of George II). These gates have been the main approach to the palace since it was opened to the public by Queen Victoria in 1838.

The Maze, Hampton Court Palace, *c.* 1910. The world-famous maze was planted in 1702. Originally, in the time of Henry VIII, the Great Orchard filled the land on the north side of the palace. In the reign of William III the entire area was laid out with hedges in geometric patterns and the maze is the sole remainder of this planting. It covers an area of a quarter of an acre in a triangular shape, with the base of the triangle being about 220 feet long and the walks totalling about half a mile.

The Lion Gates, Hampton Court Palace, *c.* 1910. The Lion Gates are located on the north side of the palace. In the time of William and Mary a new grand entrance was planned. It had been intended to demolish all the Tudor palace except the Great Hall. The new northern approach was to be formed by Chestnut Avenue in Bushy Park, sweeping around the Diana Fountain and entering the palace through the Lion Gate and Wilderness to a new Northern Court. Although Chestnut Avenue was planted in 1699 the scheme, as far as the northern façade of the palace was concerned, was never completed.

Houseboat moored at Hampton Court, *c.* 1910. The houseboats were mainly used as weekend retreats or during the summer for holidays. Locally they were moored just below Hampton Court Bridge on the Surrey side of the river, as shown here (as well as a cluster around Tagg's Island). The houseboats below the bridge were given notice to quit in 1931 due to the imminent construction of the new bridge (opened 1933) and the consequent diversion of the rivers Mole and Ember that was necessary to accommodate the alignment of the new bridge.

FURTHER READING

BOTLHS denotes Borough of Twickenham Local History Society

Atkins, Frank, *A Short Guide to the Parish Church of St Mary the Virgin*, various editions.

Beckles Willson, Anthony, *Strawberry Hill – A History of the Neighbourhood*, 1991.

Beckles Willson, Anthony, *Mr Pope and Others at Cross Deep, Twickenham in the Eighteenth Century*, 1996.

Borough of Twickenham Local History Society, *Twickenham 1600–1900: People and Places* (BOTLHS 47), 1981.

Borough of Twickenham Local History Society, *Twickenham As It Was* (Hendon), 1982.

Borough of Twickenham Local History Society, *Old Hampton, Hampton Hill and Hampton Wick* (Hendon), 1982.

Borough of Twickenham Local History Society, *Bygone Twickenham* (Hendon), 1983.

Bunch, Maureen, *Cambridge Park, Twickenham and its Owners 1616–1835* (BOTLHS 63), 1989.

Bunch, Maureen, *Cambridge Park, East Twickenham, The Building of a Suburb* (BOTLHS 68), 1992.

Cashmore, T.H.R., *York House Twickenham* (BOTLHS Occasional Paper 4), 1990.

Cashmore, T.H.R., *Orleans Family in Twickenham 1800–1932* (BOTLHS 49), reprinted 1997.

Chaplin, Peter, *The Thames at Hampton*, 1967.

Cherry, Mike, Howe, Ken and Sheaf, John, *Twickenham, Teddington & Hampton in Old Photographs* (Sutton Publishing), 1996.

Ching, Pamela, *Teddington in 1800 – The Year of the Enclosure* (BOTLHS 51), 1983.

Ching, Pamela, *The History of the Roads of Teddington* (Teddington Society), 1989.

Garside, Bernard, *A Brief History of Hampton School, 1557–1957*, 1957.

Gascoigne, Bamber and Ditchburn, Jonathan, *Images of Twickenham* (St Helena Press), 1981.

GLC, *Alexander Pope's Villa* (Exhibition Catalogue), 1980.

Heath, Gerald, *The Formation of the Local Boards of Twickenham, Teddington, Hampton and Hampton Wick* (BOTLHS 10), 1967.

Heath, Gerald, *Hampton in the Nineteenth Century* (BOTLHS 27), 1993, 2nd edn.

Howe, Ken, *Teddington – Past and Present* (Hendon), 1994.

Law, Ernest, *A Short History of Hampton Court*, 1st edn, 1897.

McCutcheon Nelson, Helen and Pearce, Brian Louis, *The Happiest Days . . . A History of Education in Twickenham 1645–1918* (BOTLHS 70), 1994.

McCutcheon Nelson, Helen, *The Happiest Days . . . A History of Education in Twickenham Part II: Twentieth-century Schools* (BOTLHS 73), 1995.

Mercer, G.E., *The Cole Papers* (BOTLHS 56), 1985.

Mumford, Adrian and Simpson, Donald, *Organs of St Mary's Parish Church* (St Mary's), 1996.

Orton, Margery (ed.), *The Birth and Growth of Hampton Hill*, 1965.

Ripley, Henry, *The History and Topography of Hampton-on-Thames*, 1883.

Sheaf, John and Howe, Ken, *Hampton and Teddington Past* (Historical Publications), 1995.

Sheaf, John, *Edwardian Hampton; The Story of Hampton and Hampton Hill from 1900–1914* (BOTLHS 76), 1997.

Simpson, Donald, *Twickenham Past* (Historical Publications), 1993.

Teddington Society, *Teddington As It Was* (Hendon), 1980.

Thames Valley Times, various issues

Thurley, Simon, *Hampton Court Palace Souvenir Guide*, 1992, 2nd edn.

Urwin, Alan, *Twickenham Park*, 1965.

Urwin, Alan, *Railshead*, 1974.

Urwin, Alan, *Commercial Nurseries and Market Gardens* (BOTLHS 50), 1982.

Urwin, Alan, *The Rabbit Warrens of Twickenham* (BOTLHS 58), 1986.

Victoria County History of Middlesex, Vols II and III.

White, Kathy and Foster, Peter, *Bushy Park, Royals, Rangers and Rogues* (Foundry Press), 1997.

Windsor, Fred, *The Dream Palaces of Richmond upon Thames*. (Birmingham Mercia Cinema Society, Publications Group), 1984.

Yates, Edward, *Hampton Court*, 1935.

INDEX

TEDDINGTON, RIVERSIDE, HAMPTON WICK AND BUSHY PARK

HAMPTON, HAMPTON HILL AND HAMPTON COURT